My little s

by Jenny Giles
Photography by Bill Thomas

My little sister looks like me,
and I look like her.

I am big,
and my sister is little.
She is three.

After school,
I play with my little sister.
She likes to go up and down
on the swing.

My little sister
likes to play in the sandbox
with the cars and trucks.

I make sandcastles for her
with a bucket.

I can make a playhouse
for my little sister.

We make beds
for her teddy bears and dolls.

We look at some books
in our playhouse,
and I read to my sister.
She is too little
to read the words.

My little sister goes to sleep
with her toys
in the playhouse.

15

I look after my little sister.